THE
HUMAN
ENVIRONMENT
AND BUSINESS

THE
HUMAN
ENVIRONMENT
AND BUSINESS

HENRY FORD II
Chairman, Ford Motor Company

INTRODUCTION BY
KINGMAN BREWSTER, JR.
President, Yale University

70-3404

Weybright and Talley
NEW YORK

CONTENTS

Introduction by
Kingman Brewster, Jr., President,
Yale University   7

1.
The Individual and the Establishment   13

2.
Social Conscience and Profit   27

3.
Business, the Environment,
and the Quality of Life   45

INTRODUCTION

→≫ Verbal bluntness and practical bold- ≪← ness are the marks of these three pieces by Henry Ford II. Both qualities should be refreshing to his young audiences and to readers of any age.

His bluntness is in happy contrast to the artful double-talk which comes from the effort to please everybody. Ambiguity is not a happy nor a respected refuge. And literary persiflage is not a successful camouflage for the lack of ideas. Here there is an honest effort to "tell it like it ought to be" even if that is sometimes different from "telling it like it is." Politicians, commencement speakers, hucksters everywhere would do well to take a leaf, any leaf, from this book.

The boldness is welcome relief from the blandness of those carefully couched phrases which are designed, as the saying goes, "to preserve the options." The style as well as the substance of these lectures reminds the reader that risk, and the gleeful willingness to take risk, are essential to the capitalist promise. Hedging or fudging the alternatives is not Mr. Ford's style. After so much in our image-made society that is "on the one hand and on the other" it is refreshing to see affirmations unqualified.

At the same time the boldness is practical. Its practicality is not only the practicality of a man of action, it is the realism of a person who knows that posturing and sloganeering are no substitute for dealing with the complex and often contradictory realities. Someone whose life is devoted to making things happen somehow conveys the practical sense that you don't move the checkers across the board by theorizing about the next move or by ignoring the practical difficulties which any step forward involves.

So, boldness is free of the hedging of the timid, but it is also practical in its refusal to ignore reality or to claim too much.

Such is the flavor I get out of these essays. They ring with the boldness and bluntness which is the human mark of their author, not

8

a man much given either to patience or to circumlocution. As someone said of another friend of mine, he speaks with "a bluntness which defies misunderstanding."

And what does all this abstract comment mean in terms of what Mr. Ford is trying to say? Well, my short instinct is to reply, simply: read them and find out.

The first talk, given at Vanderbilt, is a hard-headed analysis of the options which are open to the young. Restlessness is welcomed, provided it bespeaks a willingness to shoulder the job of turning its energy to constructive account. The lure of some "easy" way to be useful is scorned by the challenge of constructive action—more challenging because it is tough.

The second, given, I'm proud to say, at the invitation of the Yale students' Political Union, reaffirms the value and essentiality of the profit motive if private business is to do its job in the public interest. At the same time it eschews the soft notion that the public responsibility of private enterprise and power can somehow be discharged as a tithe to ethics and charity. It urges, rather, a broader self-interest, profitable self-interest, which insists that policies, practices, and resources of private enterprise should be positively devoted to the eradication of racial exclusion, oppression, and poverty.

9

The third, given, with a tinge of humility, to a Harvard Business School audience, walks straight and uncringing up to the demands of the society and the natural environment upon private industrial enterprise. It also accepts the inevitable role of government. Both the stick of regulation and the carrot of public financial incentive to socially useful behavior are welcomed.

Maybe it was in part the "put up or shut up" goad of his own words which led the author not too long after the Harvard speech, to lay it on the line in terms of Ford Motor Company's dedication of millions to invest in the eradication of polluted exhaust from new automobiles.

Unless I miss my bet, one of the big questions ahead is whether free market capitalism—with all its virtues as a way of allocating benefits and burdens through an impersonal competitive market, and its incentives to fantastic innovation—can cope with environmental and qualitative demands, which do not register themselves in terms of price, productivity, or profit.

Mr. Ford is insistently optimistic that enlightened corporate self-interest will solve the problem. While I agree that business has a very great self-interest in making the market responsible in order to keep it free, I think that there is a challenge to legal ingenuity as well as to executive motivation.

On the one hand direct subsidies or indirect subsidies by way of tax incentive may well raise the profit without returning the gain to the public if they are made generally available. The history of percentage depletion is not a comforting analogy. On the other hand subsidies or tax favors which are administered or negotiated ad hoc (such as accelerated amortization on Reconstruction Finance Corporation loans) are wide open to political and administrative favoritism.

The regulatory route is no happier. The public red tape of bureaucracy and the private red tape of litigatory obstruction are an unhappy price to pay in order to harness private initiative to the public interest.

These lectures do serve to open the challenge, for the public interest would be less if private initiative had to be choked in the name of public objectives.

Kingman Brewster, Jr.
President, Yale University

THE
INDIVIDUAL
AND THE
ESTABLISHMENT

Remarks delivered at the Vanderbilt Forum, Vanderbilt University, March 6, 1969.

1.

»» This evening I am going to ignore «« the generation gap and discuss with you some aspects of the extraordinary ferment in American education and society. The eruptions of student violence which monopolize the headlines are, it seems to me, only the visible tip of an enormous iceberg. Student discontent and activism are widespread—even worldwide—and are now reaching down into secondary schools. In the United States, the student rebellion is closely linked with the urban crisis, the war against poverty, the struggle for civil rights, the rise of black nationalism, and opposition to the Vietnam war.

Young people, black people and draft resistors are not, however, the only rebels. Police-

men, firemen, teachers, and other public ser-
vants are organizing and striking. Union members overrule union leaders. Taxpayers vote
down tax increases. Servicemen challenge mili-
tary discipline, while priests defy bishops and
bishops, the Vatican.

Even the industrial establishment is vulner-
able. In the automobile industry, we have long
been accustomed to dealing with organized
labor. Now we are also confronted by dealers
who are discontented with their relations with
the factory, by rebellious customers who are dissatisfied with products and service, and by irate
citizens who are disturbed by air pollution,
traffic accidents, traffic congestion, and highway
construction.

At a different level, sexual values are also
being revolutionized. Traditional standards of
virtue, modesty, and propriety are changing
with bewildering speed and so are the cultural
distinctions between male and female. At the
University of Michigan, we now have a co-ed
organization which, for want of a better name,
still calls itself a fraternity. Since changes such
as these go to the root of family life and social
structure, they are perhaps as important as any
I have mentioned.

There are, in my judgment, two equally valid
ways of summing up these developments. On the

one hand, it seems clear that much of the civilized world is facing a crisis of confidence. For a large and growing number of people, loyalty to institutions and obedience to written and unwritten laws are no longer automatic. However one may feel about specific issues, this general trend is terribly dangerous. Unless the great majority of citizens are willing to govern themselves by generally accepted standards, the only alternatives are chaos or a police state which governs by force and by fear.

The other way of looking at the spreading spirit of rebellion is much more hopeful. Throughout the world, ordinary people, especially young people, are deciding that they have had it with the way things are. They are no longer willing to put up with rules and conditions which make life more narrow and less satisfying than it could be. They want a voice in decisions which affect them. They are more concerned with the quality of life and their relations with people than with the quest for status and possessions.

From this point of view, the spirit of rebellion is a reaffirmation of the human spirit. It is a demand for independence and an attack on tyranny of all kinds. However one may feel about specific issues, this trend holds great hope of building a better world, a more pleasant environment, a more just social order and greater freedom for the individual.

I believe our country, along with many others, is approaching a turning point. The growing spirit of rebellion could ruin us or save us. It could drag us down into chaos and repression. Or it could lead us on to greater human freedom and fulfillment than we can now even imagine.

Whether we take the one route or the other depends on how we respond, as a people, to the nearly universal conviction that the world is not as it should be.

One possible response is to accept the world as it is, to conform meekly to all its defects and to pretend that things are better than they are. This, I suspect, is what most young people think their parents have done—and in part they may be right.

A second response is to write off the larger world and withdraw to a small and private world of self-indulgence.

A third response is to condemn society in all its works and parts and to seek to tear down everything in preparation for a fresh start.

A fourth possible response is to start with what we have and to work from within to build something better.

I need not waste words on the first two possibilities. Conformity and withdrawal are equally negative choices and neither is worth further consideration.

The most conclusive argument against revolution is that it is not really possible. Great universities and major cities can in fact be brought to a halt by the violence of a small minority. But the more often this happens, the more vigorously it will be repressed. If violence continues to spread, its only accomplishment will be to create a society in which no man is safe either from the tyranny of government or the tyranny of the mob.

This brings us to the fourth and last response to the conviction that the world is not as it should be—the possibility of starting with what we have and working from within to build something better.

Many of the young people I have talked to have grave doubts about whether the fourth way is still possible. They look about and see a society composed of huge, impersonal, hierarchical institutions—big universities, big business, big labor, big government. They believe, correctly, that big institutions have a built-in tendency to become rigid, arbitrary and unresponsive.

Young people feel themselves under pressure to live by rules they did not make and which no one can explain or justify to their satisfaction. The power to change the rules seems out of reach. The knowledge required to understand—much less control—our complex, technological society seems impossible to master. This is supposed to be a democracy, but how can we have a democracy if only the experts know the answers?

In circumstances like these, young people wonder if there is really any room left to be one's self and to affect the way things are. These are real questions that should be raised and deserve to be answered.

My answer would be this. It is now, and it always has been, enormously difficult to live and work with other people and still be true to yourself. It is, and always has been, even more difficult to affect the way things are— to change the complex web of rules and sanctions that hold a society together. Difficult, yes, but impossible, no; and in some ways it is less difficult now than ever before.

It is less difficult, for one thing, because our society has never been more tolerant of diversity and dissent in speech and behavior. Young people may still feel oppressed by too many unnecessary rules. To those whose memories are just a little longer, however, it is plain that people can now say and do things that would not have been tolerated only a few years ago.

The progress of the numerous rebel causes I listed earlier is both a proof and a source of this new freedom.

In the past, we have always asked: How much freedom can we afford to grant? Now many people are asking a new question: How many restrictions on freedom are really necessary? Until we reach a new consensus in answer to this new question, we are bound to have trouble and turmoil. Some are bound to feel that freedom has gone too far; others, that it has not gone far enough. But I , for one, believe that now, at last, we are beginning to ask the right question.

The men who manage large institutions— school administrators, business executives, government officials—have been forced to recognize that they need to be more responsive to people and more sensitive to their drive for self-determination. Universities like Vanderbilt are giving students more voice in decisions and more freedom in their private lives. Companies like Ford are now paying starting salaries in five figures to ambitious, talented young people with advanced degrees. These young people won't tolerate being treated like cogs in a machine. We can't afford to treat them that way because they can always leave, and because we need them more than they need us.

The opportunity to leave and go someplace else is another example of how it is becoming easier, in some ways, to be true to yourself. Participatory democracy is a popular concept among young people these days—the idea that the only way an individual can really be free is to have a voice in, or even a veto over, all the decisions that affect him. Participatory democracy is fine in theory, but hard to put into practice.

A much more workable way to find personal freedom is to go someplace else if you don't like the decisions where you are. No society has ever offered the individual more places to go—more options as to the kind of life he leads and the kind of work he does. Our country offers such diversity, mobility and abundant employment opportunity that no one with reasonable expectations has to live in a community or work in a job that displeases him—especially if he is a college graduate.

The freedom of choice our country offers springs largely from the technology, the affluence and the business growth which young liberals often disdain. There's an old saying that time is money. It's just as correct the other way around: Money is time and mobility and the freedom to do what you want to do.

This, of course, is not a full answer to the

doubts that young people have about their place in the scheme of things. They want more than the freedom to choose. They also want to feel that they can have some control over events and some power to help make the world a better place for other people as well as for themselves. I believe you have much more power than you think.

It's true that events are hard to control and reform is difficult to achieve. But the basic reason why reform comes slowly is not that it is blocked by the concentration of power in the hands of a reactionary establishment. The basic reason is exactly the opposite. The reason is that nobody—not the chancellor of Vanderbilt or the chairman of Ford or the President of the United States—has enough power to set things straight in a hurry.

Nothing ever changes very much because someone with a big title issues an order. Orders always have to be carried out by stubborn and unpredictable people. Unless these people agree with the order, either nothing much happens, or something happens that is quite different from the intent of the order.

It works the other way around, too. If enough people are strongly convinced that something needs to be changed, the people with titles have to respond in order to retain their positions and their effectiveness. When students feel strongly that university rules should be changed, changes begin to happen. When citizens decide that something has to be done about traffic accidents and air pollution, something is done.

Power is never monopolized by a few people at the top. Important changes almost always occur in little steps as a result of the complex interaction of many people at many levels all pulling in somewhat different directions. Everyone who pulls has some influence on the outcome and some share of the power.

Let me make one other comment on the relationship of the establishment to the high hopes and ideals of young people. I think you would be surprised if you knew how many establishment people share your views about what is wrong with society and your hopes for improvement. *Fortune* magazine recently reported the results of a survey which asked businessmen to name the most important goals the new administration should pursue. The three most important goals, in the opinion of businessmen, are: One, end the war. Two, curb inflation without causing high unemployment. Three, devote more resources and attention to the problems of the cities and the poor.

Your own list might be somewhat different,

but I think most of you would agree that these are important and worthy goals. This, it seems to me, is a sign that it is indeed possible for you to find a place within the system and still be true to yourselves and your ideals.

It is not easy to be an independent individual and an effective member of society. But it is possible. To build a good life for yourself takes the initiative to find the niche in the world that is best suited to your personal interests and abilities. To have an influence on events, it is necessary to work with others who share your hopes and are pulling in roughly the same direction. To work with others and still be true to yourself requires a delicate balance between independence and self-assertion, on the one hand, and cooperation and self-restraint, on the other.

Working with others takes the grace to accept direction, compromise, delay and even defeat. To be independent one must have at the same time the strength to maintain one's own standards of right and wrong, the patience to persist, the skill to persuade and motivate others, and the knowledge to come up with the best answers.

These are qualities that do not emerge spontaneously. They have to be developed by hard work and long practice. But the prize is worth the effort. If enough of your generation are willing to make the effort, you can do more for yourselves and the world than any previous generation has ever been able to accomplish.

Whether the spirit of rebellion abroad in the world leads to chaos and tyranny or to the liberation of the human spirit is in your hands.

SOCIAL
CONSCIENCE
AND
PROFIT

Remarks delivered before the Yale Political Union at
Yale University, April 17, 1969.

2.

→>> A great deal has changed since my last ⟨⟨
visit to Yale ten years ago, and almost
everything has changed since I was a student
here some thirty years ago. But there are some
things about Yale that never change and I still
feel very much at home.

Ten years ago, college students were
described as the silent generation and the
fashionable theme for campus speeches was
to appeal to the young to become more
committed, more concerned and more active
in the problems of the world. Today, most of
those speakers probably wish that they had
left well enough alone.

Perhaps they can take some comfort in the

thought that their appeals for action probably had as little impact on the students of the fifties as their appeals for restraint appear to be having on the students of the sixties.

My starting point here, however, is not the role of students in building a better world, but the role of business. How much business can and should do to solve the problems of society is currently the subject of a lively debate. The answers range from everything to nothing. The real answer, in my opinion, is somewhere in between. Business can and should do something, but far from everything.

Like governments and universities and other institutions, business is much better at some tasks than at others. Business is especially good at all the tasks that are necessary for economic growth and development. To the extent that the problems of society can be solved by providing more and better jobs, higher incomes for more people and a larger supply of goods and services, the problems can best be solved by relying heavily on business.

On the other hand, business has no special competence in solving many other urgent problems. Businessmen, for example, know little about the problems involved in improving the education of ghetto children, the quality of ghetto family life, the relations between police and minority citizens or the administration of justice. Solutions to problems such as these will be more effective if they are left to political, educational and social agencies. In short, our society will be served best if each of its specialized institutions concentrates on doing what it does best, and refuses either to waste its time or to meddle in tasks it is poorly qualified to handle.

I can best illustrate these broad generalizations by discussing the role of business in solving one of the nation's most urgent problems —the problem of providing equal economic opportunity for Negroes, Indians, Spanish-speaking Americans and other disadvantaged peoples. Since this is largely an economic problem, I believe that business has a large role in solving it.

Not everyone agrees with me. Oddly enough, the extreme left and the extreme right agree with each other that the profit motive rules out any significant contribution by business to the solution of the economic problems of disadvantaged peoples. The right says that business *should* concern itself exclusively with maximizing profit. It regards any special effort to help minorities as discrimination in reverse and a violation of management's obligations to the stockholder.

The left, on the other hand, says that business *does* concern itself exclusively with profit and therefore will never really do anything to help people who need help. Many on the far left go on to say that business deliberately exploits and oppresses the disadvantaged in order to increase its profits. Colonialism at home, they believe, is the main reason for poverty and the main bulwark of prejudice.

Both of these views can be refuted by the same answer. I agree with the right that business *should* concern itself primarily with profit. I agree with the left that business *does* concern itself primarily with profit. But neither premise supports the conclusion that business has no role in promoting equal opportunity. On the contrary, even if there were no other reason, business should have a role because equal opportunity is profitable.

There are, of course, some businessmen who profit from prejudice and poverty. Blockbusting real estate operators, loan sharks, and unscrupulous landlords are among the obvious examples. These, however, are the exceptions rather than the rule. The rule is that people who have money, education, and opportunity make better customers, better employees, and better neighbors for business than people who are poor, ignorant, and oppressed.

It is clearly in the self-interest of businessmen to enlarge their markets by selling housing, insurance, credit, restaurant meals, haircuts, automobiles, and all other products and services to all comers on equal terms. Any businessman who discriminates against certain classes of customers automatically reduces his sales and profits. Whenever discrimination against disadvantaged customers is widespread, the only people who benefit, as I've just pointed out, are the few businessmen who specialize in serving such markets at higher prices.

It is clearly in the self-interest of business both to enlarge its markets and to improve its work force by helping disadvantaged people to develop and employ their economic potential. Good employees are any company's most valuable resource. Good employees are also hard to find. Any company that limits its access to good employees by imposing such irrelevant criteria as race or color is also limiting its profit potential.

Likewise, it is in the self-interest of business to help reduce dependency, frustration, crime and conflict in the community by treating all people on their merits as individuals. The costs of occasional civil disorder are impossible to overlook, but are far smaller than the continuing costs of welfare, crime, disease and waste of human potential—costs which are borne by business as well as by the rest of the community.

In short, the profit motive provides abundant incentive for businessmen to help solve the economic problems of the disadvantaged.

I will readily admit that business did not move soon enough and has not moved far enough to provide full equality of opportunity. But we have not lagged *because* of the profit motive. We have lagged *in spite of* the profit motive and in opposition to our own best interests.

Businessmen have lagged because they are people who share the prejudices and preconceptions of the society around them. Like other people, businessmen are reluctant to change the way things have always been done. In a community where Negroes have never been hired except as janitors or sweepers, it takes an exceptional man to break the pattern.

If businessmen are no better than other people, they are also no worse. Like the rest of American society, American business is now waking up to its own self-interest in doing what is right. The stirrings of conscience have led us to see our own interests in a clearer light and we are now acting more decisively.

The idea that conscience and profit pull in the same direction is a difficult one to accept.

34

There is something in human nature which makes us feel that profit is a poor reason for helping others. But this is a feeling we should resist. To help a man because we think it is good for him is to treat him as an inferior. It is difficult to do good without being condescending and paternalistic and perpetuating dependence. To hire a man because he needs a job rather than because the job needs him is to assure him that he is useless.

On the other side of the coin, to help a man because it is in your own interest to help him is to treat him as an equal. It is a way of telling him that you have confidence in him and in his ability to stand on his own feet and take care of his own interests.

Self-interest is also a more reliable motive than altruism. Negroes and other disadvantaged people have learned from bitter experience that promises of help are often much bigger than performance. They are justifiably suspicious of white liberals who are better at starting programs than they are at finishing them. Today they suspect that business programs to hire and upgrade the disadvantaged are a fad that will fade away with little accomplishment. The best assurance that this will not happen is the recognition by businessmen that equal opportunity is profitable.

What I am suggesting is simply that good results are much more valuable than good intentions. Like most other big companies Ford has established its good intentions with respect to equal opportunity and made them a part of its basic corporate policy. We have devoted much effort to carrying out that policy, but our results, like those of most other companies, are still very mixed.

Our biggest results have been in providing entry-level production jobs for the so-called hard-core unemployed. Negroes and other disadvantaged people have always been an important part of our work force, but since late 1967 we have deliberately recruited people who would have been rejected as poor employment risks in the past. So far, we have hired some 12,000 of them.* We have found among them some outstanding employees and on the average they have been about as satisfactory in most respects as other new employees hired during the same period. Negroes and other minorities now make up more than 25 percent of our hourly work force in the U.S. compared with 18 percent five years ago.

Many other employers have achieved similar results. The National Alliance of Businessmen was formed early in 1968 to work with the

* By February, 1970, Ford had hired 20,000.

federal government to encourage employers to hire the hard-core unemployed. By the end of the year, the Alliance had placed 125,000 people in jobs with 12,500 firms and 85,000 of those hired were still on the job.*

At Ford, we have also done fairly well in giving minorities access to entry-level salaried positions. We have done less well in raising them to positions as plant foremen and skilled workers.

In other areas, we have barely scratched the surface. We have very few Negroes and other minorities in the higher salaried positions. We have only four Negro dealers—which is four more than we had a couple of years ago—and there are very few in the dealer sales force. We have a program to support the development of minority businesses through our purchasing activities, but so far it has hardly gotten off the ground. In each of these areas, although our results are still small, our progress is accelerating.†

We intend to continue increasing our rate of progress, but our results will depend more on hard work and good management than on

* By January 31, 1970, NAB placements had reached 380,000, of whom 200,000 were still on the job.

† Three more Negro-owned dealerships had been added by early 1970.

good intentions. To translate any set of intentions into results, programs have to be developed and built into the structure of the organization and its operating procedures. We need to make changes in our organization, to allocate responsibility and authority, to determine priorities, establish targets, timetables and reporting procedures, make up budgets, provide incentives and do all the numerous things a big organization needs to do to reach any goal. In the past, our equal opportunity efforts have been scattered and largely uncoordinated. Now we are getting ourselves better organized to translate our intentions into accomplishments in every aspect of our business.

There has been a great deal of discussion about whether or not it is proper to discriminate in favor of minorities in order to make up for generations of discrimination against them. In my opinion, much of this argument is academic. There is still a long way to go in eliminating discrimination *against* before we have to start worrying too much about discrimination *for*.

I am not talking so much about out-and-out racial prejudice, which is no longer the main problem in most big companies. Rather, I am talking about a variety of practices and procedures which have the effect of discriminating against even though their purpose is pure.

The purpose of educational requirements for employment, for example, is to select employees who will be able to perform well in particular jobs. The theory is that a man's future job performance can be predicted from past performance and experience in school. In practice, however, the predictions often turn out to be wrong. Some people who have the required education can't do the work, and some people who can do the work don't have the required education. In routine jobs, too much education may even be a handicap, and the man with less schooling may be a better risk.

In practice, therefore, minimum educational standards for jobs always discriminate against people who could meet the job standards even though they cannot meet the education standards. Discrimination of this kind has its biggest impact on Negroes and other groups of people whose educational achievement is relatively low. Obviously, the answer to this problem is to develop innovative personnel practices which make it possible for a man to show what he can really do in spite of apparent handicaps. That's not discrimination for or against anybody. It's just common sense and fair play and self-interest.

Even when this point is reached, however, it will still be difficult to achieve big gains in minority employment in the better jobs. There is no escaping the fact that minority group members who are really qualified by skill and knowledge to handle the better jobs are very hard to find.

Industry can do something through training programs to make up for the shortage, but industry cannot handle this whole job by itself. The shortage is a reflection of the deficiencies of ghetto schools, ghetto medical care, ghetto housing and ghetto life. Before these deficiencies can be remedied, school systems, city governments and other community organizations will have to organize themselves in the same way that business is now getting organized to translate good intentions into good results.

The success of these efforts to get organized for good results will depend, in turn, on the kinds of people who are managing the organizations. No organization can be more progressive or more effective than its people. This is just as true of school systems and governments as it is of business.

This brings me, in conclusion, to your generation, to the students of today and what they can do to make the world somewhat better.

Your generation seems intensely disillusioned not only with big business but also with big universities, big government and big organizations in general. If you feel that way, I don't blame you. I can assure you—and I know that President Brewster would agree with me—that big organizations are at least as frustrating to the people who administer them as they are to the people who are affected by them.

On the other hand, we have to accept the fact that big organizations are here to stay. We cannot turn back to a simpler age and a smaller scale. We cannot decide whether or not to rely on big organizations; our only choice is whether they shall be better or worse. If the big ideals of our time are not achieved through our major institutions, they will not be achieved at all.

The great opportunity your generation faces is the opportunity to transform our major institutions and make them serve your highest ideals. If the best and most idealistic people of your generation accept this opportunity, then there is hope for a better future. But if the best of you reject business and other large organizations, then our national institutions will surely become even less effective and more stagnant than their worst critics claim they are.

In business, in government, in school systems

and in all our major institutions, we need people who are convinced that the way things are is a shame and a disgrace. It is easy to stay outside the system and protest the way it works. Protest has its place, but right now our country seems to have all the protestors it can use. What we really need are more people who are willing to come inside the system and fight and work to make the system better.

If any of you believe that our present institutions are not worth fighting and working for, let me remind you of one thing. In the perspective of history, the astonishing thing about our American institutions is not that they work so poorly. The astonishing thing is that they work as well as they do. We should count it as our great good fortune that our present institutions—for all their grave deficiencies—are perhaps the most effective that any society has ever inherited. To give up on the best because it is not better is not the counsel of idealism. It is the counsel of despair.

If any of you believe that the struggle for a better society would be hopeless and the work useless, let me remind you of another thing. It is natural for youth to be impatient for faster progress. To those of you who may feel discouraged by the slow pace of reform, I would respond that it's always hard to teach an old dog new tricks. Major progress in any field of endeavor seldom comes because people change their minds and their way of doing things. It comes because one generation grows old and leaves the field and another generation takes over.

The correct measure of possible progress in the future is not the actions of my generation, but the ambitions of yours. The size of the generation gap today suggests that when your generation takes over, the progress could really be major. How much progress big organizations can make toward building a better world is not fixed in the nature of organizations. It depends on you.

BUSINESS, THE ENVIRONMENT, AND THE QUALITY OF LIFE

Remarks delivered at the Harvard Business School Public
Affairs Forum, December 2, 1969.

3.

→>> One of the first rules of public speak- <<←
ing is to stick to subjects you know more about
than your audience does. By that rule, I'm sure
that no outsider should ever talk about business
at Harvard Business School.

In order to keep myself on a reasonably even
footing with this audience, I'm going to talk
about one aspect of business on which everyone
is as poorly informed as everyone else. I'm
going to talk, that is, about business in the
future.

The one thing we can be sure about in discussing the future is that it will be different
from the present. In a recent issue of the
Harvard Business Review, Peter Drucker ob-

served that the changes between now and the year 2000 will be as great as the changes that took place between 1860 and 1914.

That's a fairly modest forecast. Dean William Haber of the University of Michigan recently told a group of Ford executives that the year 2000 will be as different from 1969 as 1969 is from the year 1500.

I believe Dr. Haber will prove to be a better prophet than Dr. Drucker. We are living in truly revolutionary times and it is difficult to imagine the magnitude, much less the nature, of the changes that will take place during the next three decades.

In my judgment, the most important of these changes, for business, will be those involving the relationship between business firms and the society they serve. As customers, as employees, and as citizens, people are expecting many more things and very different things from business than they ever expected in the past.

The revolution in expectations has already come far enough to suggest how much farther it may go. It has already had a profound and varied impact on business costs and operations.

Let me give you a few examples from our recent experience at Ford Motor Company. We are now spending half a billion dollars a year in the United States and Canada to keep up with government standards and catch up with public expectations with respect to automotive safety and air pollution.

And that's just the beginning. Leaving safety regulations aside, concern over polluted air has led to proposals in Congress and in several state legislatures, including Massachusetts, to ban the internal combustion engine altogether, and surveys show that many people think this would be a good idea. The State of Illinois is suing the auto manufacturers to force them to install and pay for emission control devices on all the cars built since 1953. A similar suit has now been filed in New York State. However these particular efforts turn out, it is abundantly clear that the auto industry needs to develop virtually emission-free vehicles as quickly as possible.

Another set of changes in public expectations is usually described under the heading of consumerism. For the auto industry, consumerism means, first of all, a rising tide of customer impatience with the cost and inconvenience of auto repairs and services.

Dissatisfied service customers are finding a sympathetic hearing in Congress, in state legislatures and in regulatory agencies. Recently, they have found another ally—the auto insurance companies, many of which are losing money in spite of rapidly rising premiums.

Again, the lesson is clear. The auto companies will have to find ways of making faster progress in reducing the need for and the cost of auto repairs and services.

Employees, of course, were the first of our many publics to organize effectively to put pressure on management in support of their expectations. We have been dealing with unions for many years, but even in this area the seeds of change are evident. The voice of monolithic unions is made uncertain by the demands of splinter groups which are unwilling to accept the will of the union majority.

Our company, along with many others, has accepted a responsibility to modify employment practices in such a way as to help solve the national race crisis and help bring Negroes and other minorities into the mainstream of the economy. We are not only employing minorities in growing numbers, but are also implementing specific plans and programs to promote them as rapidly as possible and to help them to become successful dealers and suppliers as well as successful employees.

In the past, management has taken it for granted that there would always be an adequate supply of people willing to perform a hard day's factory work in return for a good day's wages. Now we are beginning to wonder. More and more employees and potential employees are deciding that they would rather accept less pay for easier and pleasanter work. The costs of absenteeism and turnover are rising steeply, and it is increasingly difficult to maintain plant discipline.

Even our dealers are joining the parade. They are having growing success in the courts and in state legislatures in restricting the ability of the manufacturers to influence their operations or to take corrective action when dealers fail to live up to their obligations under their franchise agreements.

The list of ways in which business costs and operations are affected by changing public expectations is almost endless. We are asked, among other things, to help control inflation, reduce the balance of payments deficit, contribute to the economic growth of the under-developed countries, subsidize the revival of public transit and get rid of junked cars.

There is, I believe, one basic reason why everyone expects more from us than ever before. We are the victims, primarily, of our own success. As the saying goes, "Man does not live by bread alone"—but he has to have the bread before he begins to think of other things. Modern industry has provided the bread in abundance, and so has made it possible for masses of people to think about what else life could offer.

As employees, people are wondering if they have given up too much of their time, their freedom and their dignity for the sake of the paycheck.

As consumers, people are realizing that affluence can be a burden. Their cars and appliances break down, their plumbing leaks, their lawns get weedy, and getting things fixed is troublesome, expensive or even impossible.

As citizens, people can see that their material possessions have been purchased at a high cost in environmental pollution—dirty air, dirty water, ugly landscape.

Modern industrial society is based on the assumption that it is both possible and desirable to go on forever providing more and more goods for more and more people. Today, that assumption is being seriously challenged. The industrial nations have come far enough down the road to affluence to recognize that more goods do not necessarily mean more happiness. They are also recognizing that more goods eventually mean more junk, and that the junk in the air, in the water and on the land could make the earth unfit for human habitation before we reach the twenty-first century.

In short, the terms of the contract between industry and society are changing. Industry has succeeded by specializing in serving one narrow segment of society's needs. We have bought labor and material and sold goods, and we have assumed that our obligations were limited to the terms of the bargain. Now we are being asked to serve a wider range of human values and to accept an obligation to members of the public with whom we have no commercial transactions. We are being asked to contribute more to the quality of life than mere quantities of goods.

Of course, these changes have been building for a long time. They are reflected in the many restrictions on business activities already imposed by legislatures, regulatory agencies and the courts. Now, because of the unprecedented growth of affluence in recent years, the changes in people's values are pressing in on us more heavily than ever—and the danger of losing our business freedom is greater than ever.

How much freedom business will retain in the closing decades of this century depends on the quality of management's response to the changing expectations of the public.

Whether inside business or outside, and whether friendly to business or hostile, most people think about these changes by dividing the responsibilities of business into two competing categories. On the one hand, there is the traditional responsibility of business to make a profit for the stockholders. On the other hand, there are the new responsibilities of business to the society at large. From this point of view, the question is: How much will business neglect one responsibility in order to serve the other?

Across the river in Cambridge, most Harvard people probably are convinced that business will never sacrifice enough profit to meet its social responsibilities adequately.

Meanwhile, some businessmen argue that the opposite is true; that business has learned to put social responsibility before profit. Sometimes businessmen, myself included, have tried to reconcile their two responsibilities by arguing that business must sacrifice profit in the short run in order to help build a healthy and grateful society that will permit higher profit in the long run. But hardly anyone disputes the proposition that service to society requires at least a short-run sacrifice of business profit.

This point of view may have been tenable in the past. As long as public expectations with respect to the social responsibilities of business were relatively narrow and modest, business could pass muster by sacrificing only a little of its short-run earnings.

Now that public expectations are exploding in all directions, we can no longer regard profit and service to society as separate and competing goals, even in the short run. The company that sacrifices more and more short-run profit to keep up with constantly rising public expectations will soon find itself with no long run to worry about. On the other hand, the company that seeks to conserve its profit by minimizing its response to changing expectations will soon find itself in conflict with all the publics on which its profits depend.

There is, however, a third alternative, and that is to stop thinking about the pursuit of profit and the pursuit of social values as separate and competing business goals.

They are not the same sort of thing at all. One is a means and one is an end, and which is which depends on where you stand. From the standpoint of business, profit is the end and public service is the means. Business earns profit by serving public needs—but profit, not service, is the goal of business. From the standpoint of society and its members, on the other hand, service is the end and profit is the means. Society gets many of its tasks done by providing profitable market opportunities—but service, not profit, is the goal of society. Whichever way you look at it, the important thing is to stop thinking that the way to increase one is to reduce the other.

This, of course, is as elementary as Economics I—but it has important implications for both business policy and government policy.

What it implies for business policy is that management should stop thinking about changing public expectations as new costs which may have to be accepted, but certainly have to be minimized. Instead, we should start thinking about changes in public values as opportunities to profit by serving new demands.

We have to ask ourselves: What do people want that they didn't want before, and how can we get a competitive edge by offering them more of what they really want? We have to think more like entrepreneurs and innovators, and less like administrators and problem solvers.

What this approach implies for government policy is that the most effective way to encourage business to serve new public needs is to rely, when possible, on market incentives. When the marketplace does not automatically translate a public need into a market demand, then government action may be required to change market conditions.

The reduction of motor vehicle emissions is an excellent example of what I have in mind.

Prior to the establishment of government emission standards, there was no market for emission control features. Although many people wanted cleaner air, individual customers would not have been willing to pay the extra cost of a low emission car because the benefits would have been imperceptible unless all customers were required to pay this cost.

When the need for abatement of air pollution was recognized, the government established realistic emission standards. By doing so, the government created a market and the auto industry has moved quickly to supply it. Within a few years, hydrocarbon emissions from new cars have been reduced by more than 80 percent, and carbon monoxide emissions have been cut by two-thirds.

Although the present system has been highly successful, it still does not make the maximum use of market incentives. Ford and other auto manufacturers are working intensively to develop vehicles with still lower emissions, but the absence of any significant market for such vehicles is a handicap. Without a market, there is no fully realistic way to test the feasibility, the acceptability and the cost of improvements, and the constructive effect of competitive pressures is weakened.

A bill has been introduced in Congress that

would help fill that void. It would require the federal government to purchase for its own use, at a premium price, vehicles which surpass current emission standards by a specified margin. Without commenting on the details of the bill, I think that this is an excellent concept.

Such legislation would not, of course, provide an immediate answer to all the technical problems that still need to be solved. If properly drawn, however, it could create a market which does not now exist. It would thereby strengthen competitive incentives and provide a realistic opportunity to test the economic and technical feasibility of incremental progress in reducing vehicle emissions. This, in turn, will provide a better basis for orderly tightening of the standards governing vehicles sold to the general public. I can promise you that when the bill is passed, and I believe it will be, Ford Motor Company will be competing vigorously in the new market it will create.

Business is always alert to market changes caused by shifts in consumer preferences. Now we face a new phenomenon—market changes caused by legislation and regulation. In the years ahead, we shall have to be as alert to these developments as we always have been to consumer desires. Whether the will of the people is expressed directly in the market, or indirectly through government, our responsibility is to earn profits by anticipating and supplying what people want.

It is clear that the American people want cleaner air, and want it very much. It doesn't take much imagination to see that before too many years have gone by, the only market left for motor vehicles will be the market for vehicles that are virtually emission-free. As a motor vehicle manufacturer, Ford's responsibility is to enhance its stockholders' investment by developing vehicles that provide the best possible combination of minimum emissions with all the other qualities people want in their cars.

Changes in the values and expectations of the public are now beginning to have an impact on automobile design that goes well beyond the addition of safety and emission control features. In the past, the American auto companies have responded to public taste by placing a heavy emphasis on styling changes and by offering steadily bigger, more luxurious, more complicated, more powerful and more costly cars.

In recent years, however, it has become apparent that these qualities have lost their appeal to a growing segment of car buyers. While many people continue to prefer big, powerful, complex cars and are willing to pay more for them, many others are more interested in ma-

neuverability, fuel economy and low mainte-
nance costs.

The Ford Maverick was designed to meet
this shift in customer preferences, and its success demonstrates the extent of the shift. The
Maverick is not just a small car with a low
price. It was deliberately designed for relia-
bility, durability, fuel economy, low mainte-
nance and repair costs, and error-free assembly
in our plants.

The market for cars with precisely these
qualities is large, growing and profitable. By
contrast with the public's interest in cleaner
air, the public's interest in reliable, economical,
trouble-free cars is automatically translated into
market demand and therefore requires no special government action. We at Ford will be
doing everything in our power to keep and
extend the lead we have established in this segment of the market, and I have no doubt that
our competitors will be doing everything they
can to cut into our lead.

Time will not permit an extended discussion
of the challenges we face in adjusting many
other aspects of our business operations to fit
the changing values and expectations of our
publics, but I would like to make a few brief
comments.

There is much truth in the charge that large

organizations like Ford Motor Company, or Harvard University for that matter, have a built-in tendency to become impersonal, inflexible and unresponsive to the needs of the individual. The evidence is piling up, however, that people are less and less willing to tolerate the frustrations that normally arise out of their relationships with large organizations.

With growing affluence, people want more out of life than just money and goods. They want freedom and dignity and leisure. They want to be treated less impersonally, more equitably, more considerately. If those of us who manage large organizations want to get more out of the people who work for us and with us, we will have to give them more of what they want. We will have to improve our relations with people across the board. We will have to listen to them, pay attention to their hopes and grievances and respond promptly and fairly. We will need to be less impersonal, more flexible and more humane.

Among other things, we will certainly have to provide genuinely equal promotional opportunities not only for Negroes and other minorities but also for women, young people, and people without college degrees—all of whom are too often discriminated against in one way or another.

In the future, management will have to put more emphasis on what individuals *actually* can do, and less emphasis on such formal criteria as education, experience, age, and sex which are intended to predict what they *probably* can do.

All of this adds up to one simple proposition: If management wants to get the most out of people, it will have to treat them as individuals. Twenty-three years ago, in one of my first public speeches, I said that if business could learn to manage people as intelligently as it managed money and facilities, American industry would enter a new era. We still have a long way to go in that direction and we have to hurry, because the people we manage are getting more and more impatient.

It should be clear to all of us that the changes my generation has lived through are nothing compared to the changes that will come during your active careers. The company that looks upon those changes as problems to solve and as costs to cut will be overwhelmed by them.

The successful companies in the last third of the twentieth century will be the ones that look at changes in their environment as opportunities to get a jump on the competition. The successful companies will be those that anticipate what their customers, their dealers, their employees and their many other publics will want in the future, instead of giving them what they wanted in the past. The successful companies will be managed by men who regard themselves as entrepreneurs, and not merely as good administrators.

These are the companies that will earn the highest profits for their stockholders by discharging their highest responsibilities to the society.